The Calligraphy of Nature

John Pearson

1817

HARPER & ROW, PUBLISHERS, INC.

New York · Cambridge · Philadelphia · San Francisco · London
Mexico · São Paulo · Sydney · Singapore

ALSO BY JOHN PEARSON
To Be Nobody Else
Kiss the Joy as It Flies
The Sun's Birthday
Begin Sweet World
Magic Doors
Love Is Most Mad and Moonly

Library of Congress Cataloging in Publication Data
Pearson, John, 1934– . The calligraphy of nature.
1. Natural history—Pictorial works. I. Title.
QH46.P38 1984   779'.3   84-47619
ISBN 0-06-091153-0 (pbk.)

Produced by Pinwheel
Calligraphy by Terry Tanaka
Book and cover design by Howard Jacobsen / Triad
Typography from Type by Design
Printed in Japan by Dai Nippon Printing Company, Ltd.

Front cover: Sunset, Mount Tamalpais, taken from the East Brother
Lighthouse, on the first clear day after a solid month of rain.

Foreword

Several years ago a man appeared in my backstage dressing room after a concert and complimented a performance of Schubert's *Shepherd on the Rock*. He said, "The music was so beautiful. I kept seeing birds, clouds, blue crystals, sea anemones. I was floating on the music." Then he handed me the book *To Be Nobody Else* and disappeared.

That was my introduction to John Pearson—photographer; minister at my wedding; godfather to my son; colleague in music and slide tours from Missoula, Montana, to the Metropolitan Museum; indefatigable punster; and author of this amazing book, *The Calligraphy of Nature*.

Why is this book special? Because it helps us look at the world as John Pearson does—lovingly, lightly, longingly, and with a twist of lemon.

I remember a call from Liz Lamson (John's wonder woman) inviting me to come along in their VW camper for a trip to some remote northern California beach where a rare minus tide was to occur extremely early the next morning. It was the middle of the night when we reached our destination. An hour or so later the alarm clock rang, and we staggered out of the camper into the dim predawn stillness of an expanse of ocean floor suddenly uncovered. I immediately began to leap from one wonder to the next watching the minus tide pools reveal their secrets.

After some time I looked around to see where John might be, and was shocked to find he had not gotten more than a few feet from the camper before kneeling in the mud all hunched over with his eye glued to his camera. I ran back to discover what it was he had seen that was so special. Incredulous, I found him staring intensely at a dumb puddle of water with no particularly interesting underwater life. "What are you doing?" I asked somewhat reproachfully. "It's the light," answered John.

Not until some weeks later could I appreciate his exclamation when I visited his home in Berkeley for an evening of slides. Extraordinary images of abstract color, shading, and motion came bursting off the screen, and I cried, "What is that?" "The minus tide," John said simply.

But it wasn't simply the minus tide—it was a magnificent translation of nature's script into calligraphy as seen through the twinkling eye of John Pearson.

These photos enrich our relationship to nature as calligraphy enhances our appreciation of the printed word. John Pearson illuminates nature's manuscript.

Richard Stoltzman

*Nature speaks to us
of our own moods –
sometimes weathered and strong...*

sometimes growing and fragile,
sometimes exposed and bare.

Nature's flow –
rhythmic, winding, wild –
nourishes us
when we are caught
in time's web.

We delight
in the music
of light
and color.

The bristlecone pine lives
by dying a little each year –
an ancient chant of 4000 years...

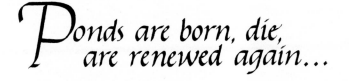

Ponds are born, die, are renewed again...

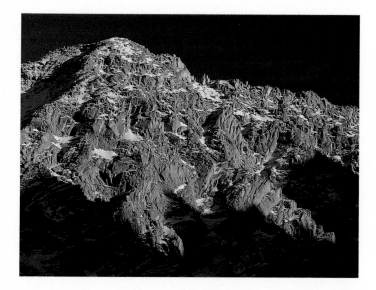

and mountains and dunes
offer an ever-changing
exhibit of light, shadow,
and color.

Cracked, caked, fragmented,
broken in a million pieces —
how often I've felt like this.
Dry spells. When will they end?

Then the ice melts, the streams flow. A quiet jubilation.

Fog
enchants
me.
It
creates
a mysterious
balance
between
reality
and
illusion.
I am
in both
worlds at
once.

*Reflections transform reality
and mirror realities within.*

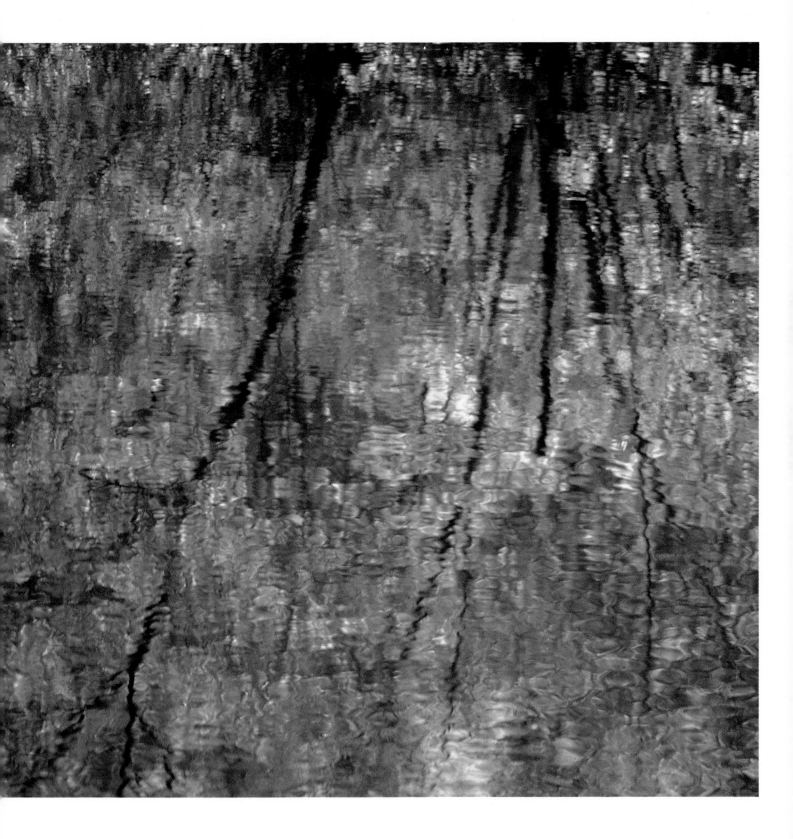

Everything in nature is in motion. Even rocks seem to flow.

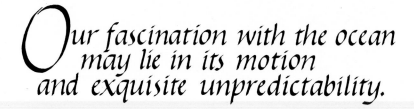

Our fascination with the ocean may lie in its motion and exquisite unpredictability.

*Light settles
on dunes and clouds
wondering where
to go next.*

*The language of light,
speaking with
eloquent silence.*

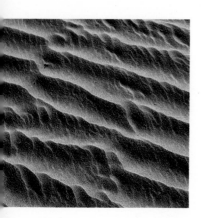  

*The language
of wind,
practicing
its calligraphy
endlessly
but playfully.*

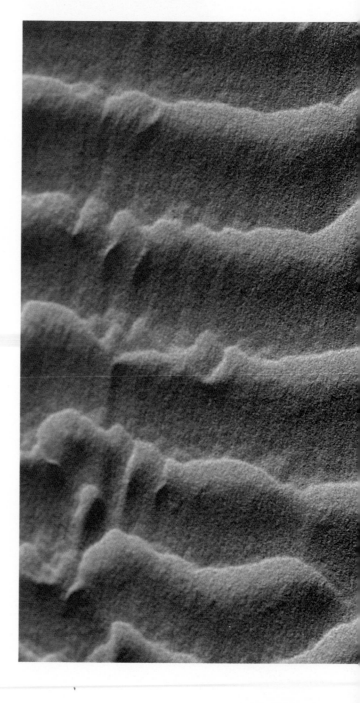

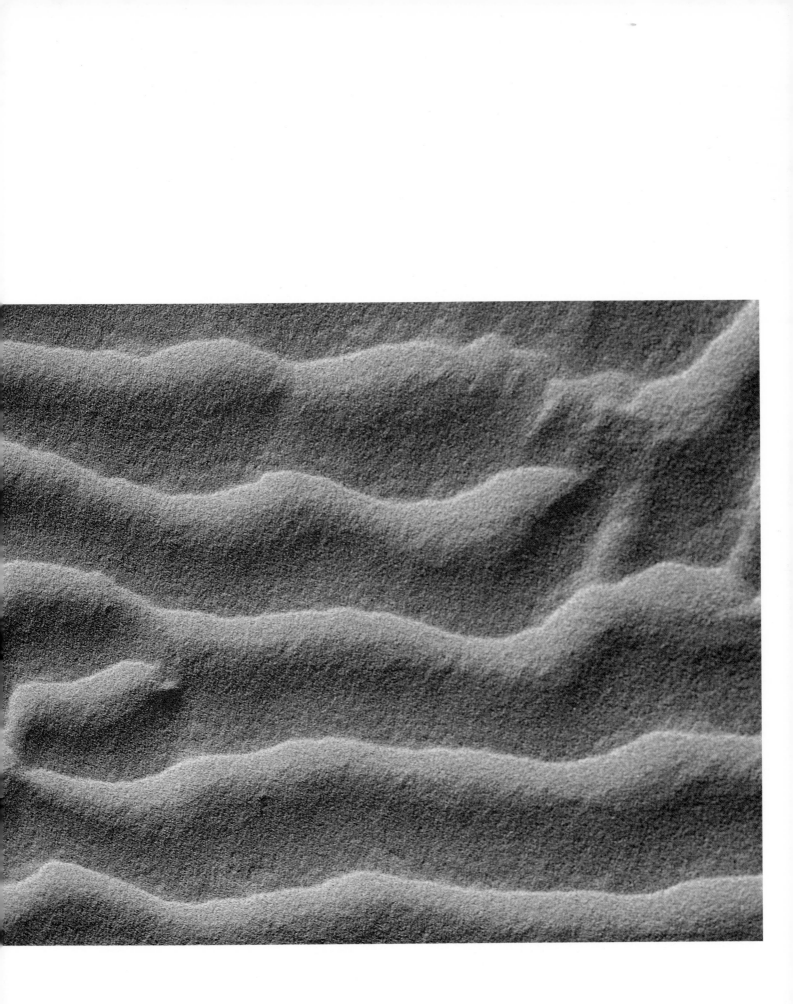

We can be soft
and translucent...

but also unyielding
and hard.

*It scares me how quickly
I can change from feeling
sparkling and self-contained...*

to fragile and blown by the winds.

*Some days I feel
sharply focused...*

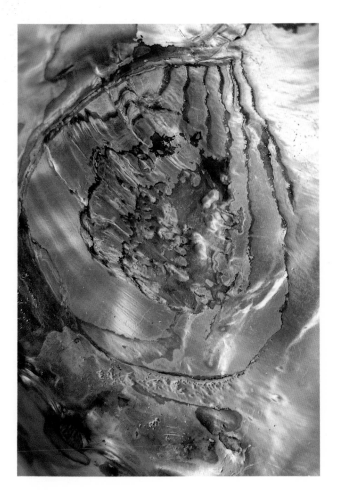

and other days
diffuse and swirling...

floating and wispy.

*S*ometimes I feel
cool and restful, waiting to thaw.
At other times
warmed, lacy, and radiant...

flaky...

or snowed under.

Canyons and caves,
almost like some subterranean brain,
the brain of the earth,
contemplating earthquakes, floods,
and flowering meadows.

The music of the spheres...

pizzicatos...

minuets…

symphonies...

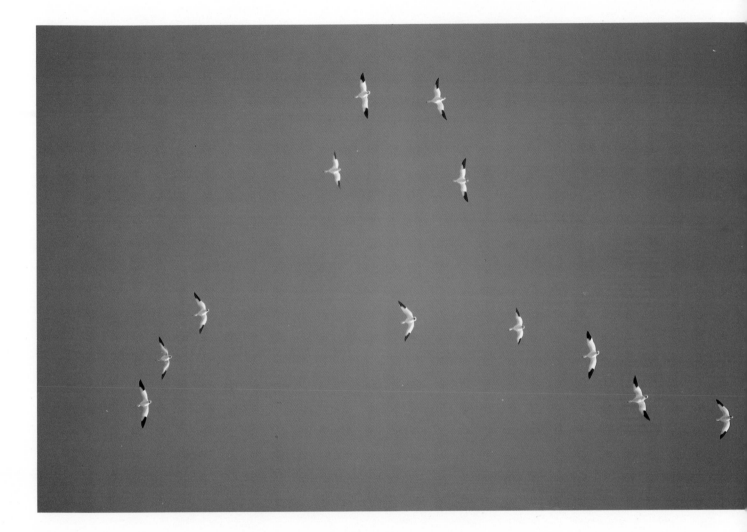

trios, quartets, and quintets.

*The calligraphy of nature
in all its beauty and power...*

is written on the sky,

written on the water,

written on the wind,

and written on us.

THE PHOTOGRAPHS

All photographs were taken in California unless otherwise noted.

EQUIPMENT: I try to keep everything as simple as I can and travel light. Most photos were taken with a 35mm single lens reflex camera hand held. I use four lenses primarily: a 35mm, a 55mm micro, an 85mm, and a 180mm. I usually use Kodachrome 25 film and occasionally Kodachrome 64. —J.P.

THANKS: Many talents were woven together to make the tapestry of this book. I would like to thank Terry Tanaka for the exquisite calligraphy, Howard Jacobsen for the beautiful design, David Barich and Kelly McCune for the excellent production, Craig Nelson and Larry Ashmead at Harper & Row, and Randy Finglund and Bill Merryman at Bookpeople. Others who have contributed in numerous ways are Tom Baird, my first photography teacher; Neil Rodman; Joe and Meri Ehrlich; Johanna and Deane Lamson; Josephine Pearson; Anne Croswell; Ed Brandstetter; Paul Duffey; Malcolm Margolin; and Lyn Sanny. Finally, my special thanks to Wayne Miller, who in 1966 suggested "a project to make you work more," which became my first book. He has been an invaluable advisor, informal editor, and friend during the last eighteen years. He has been wonderfully generous and gracious offering that delicate balance of honest criticism and hopeful encouragement.

JOHN PEARSON began photographing at age thirty, is still in love with it, and is still wondering if he can make a living at it. Most of the photographs in this book were taken "close to home" in the Bay Area and other parts of California over the last six years. Other photographs were taken in national parks, national monuments, and along back roads.

This is the first time he has combined his writing and photography. He says, "In photographing I wander around in the physical world, and in writing I wander around in the mental and spiritual world. Of course the two worlds are always flowing back and forth into each other. My hope is to feel deeply, to be surprised, and to stay connected with life itself."

The author also collaborates with musicians in performing classical and jazz "visual concerts." He performs these multi-image programs for colleges, universities, museums, community groups, and churches. He welcomes your response to this book or possible future concerts, and may be contacted by writing to P.O. Box 7516, Berkeley, California 94707.

THE AUTHOR AT WORK
Photo by Liz Lamson